Bob is a bug.

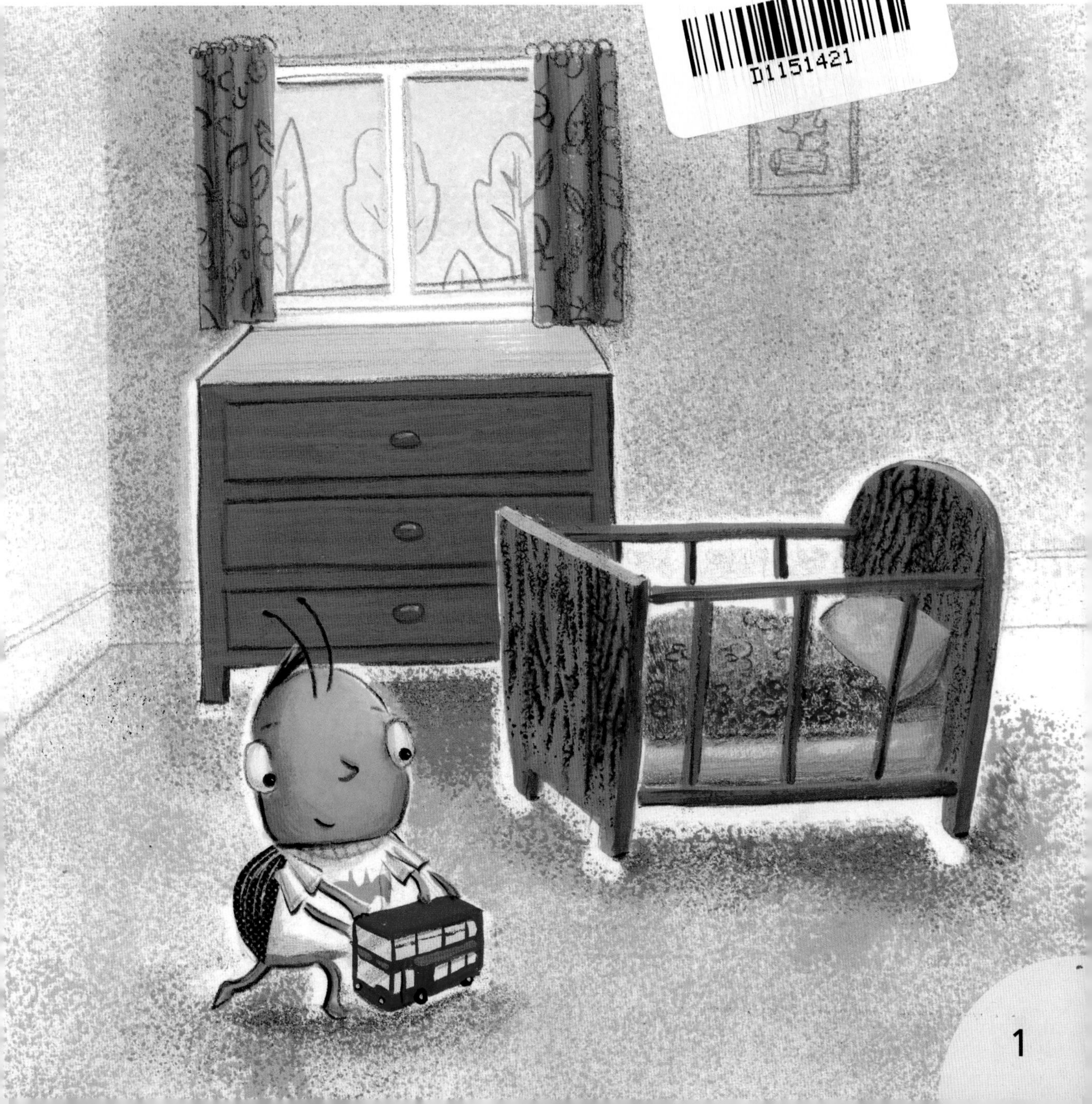

Bob Bug has a mum. His mum is big.

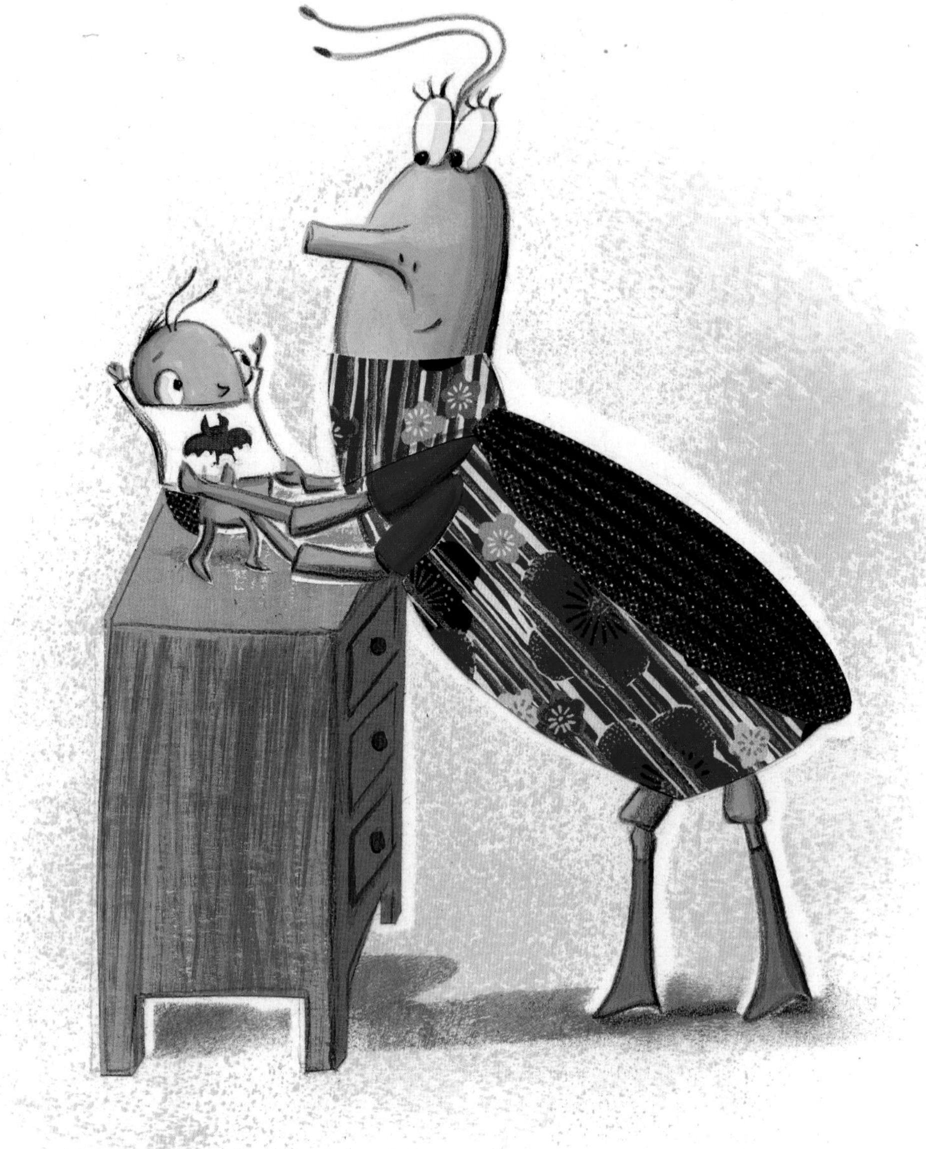

Bob has a dad. His dad is fit.

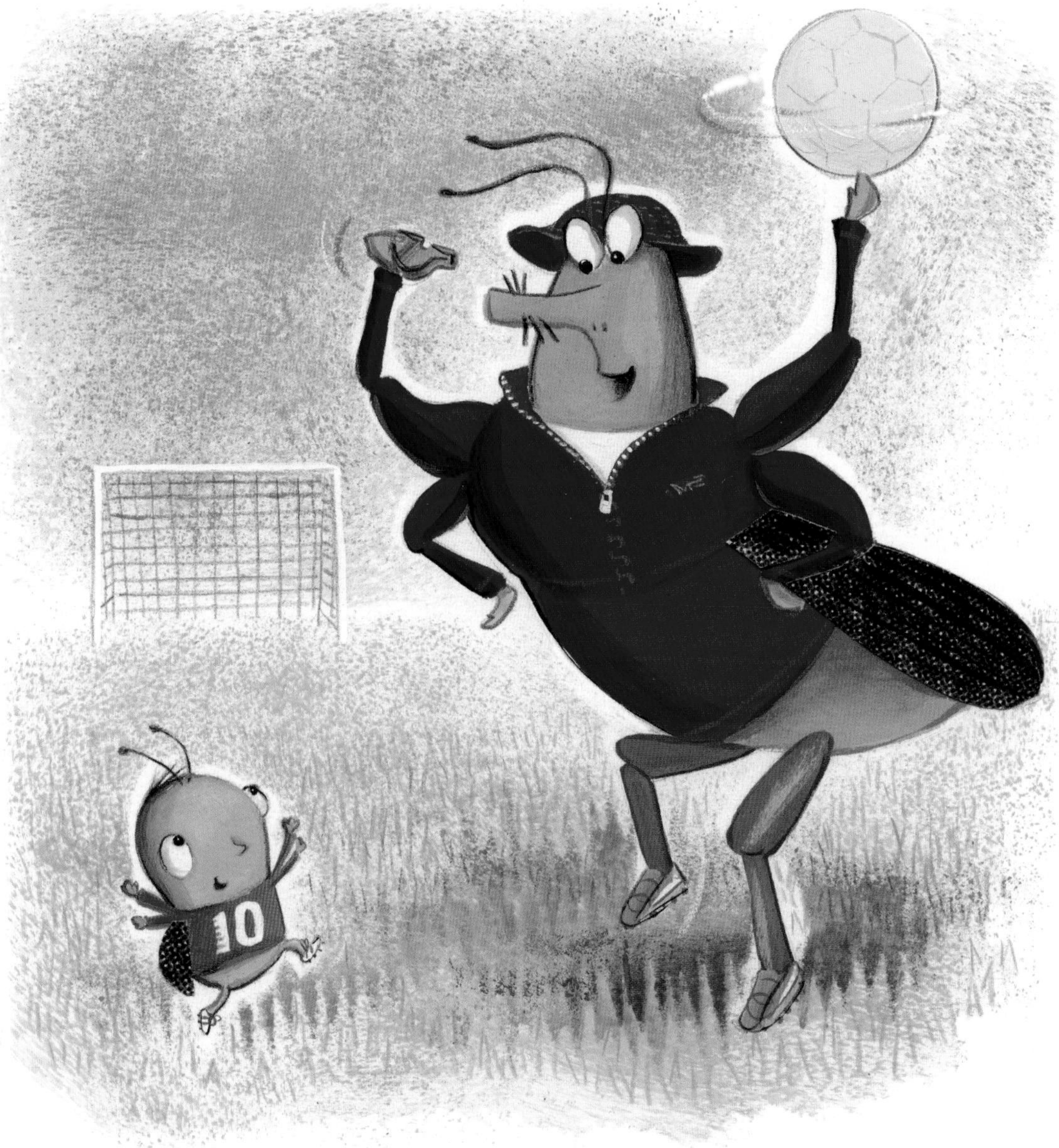

Bob has a cup. It has a lid.

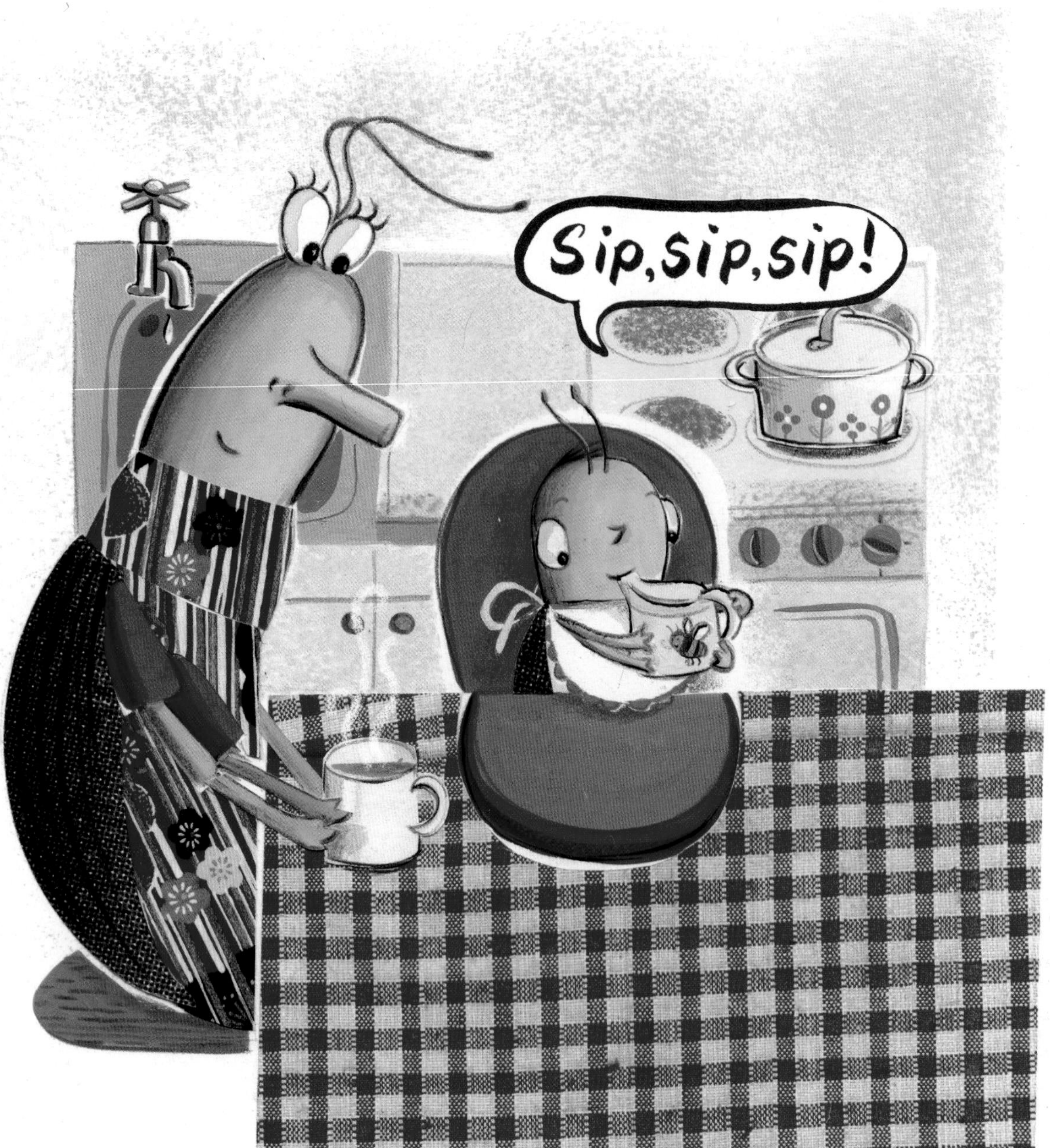

Bob has a cot. His cot has a rug.

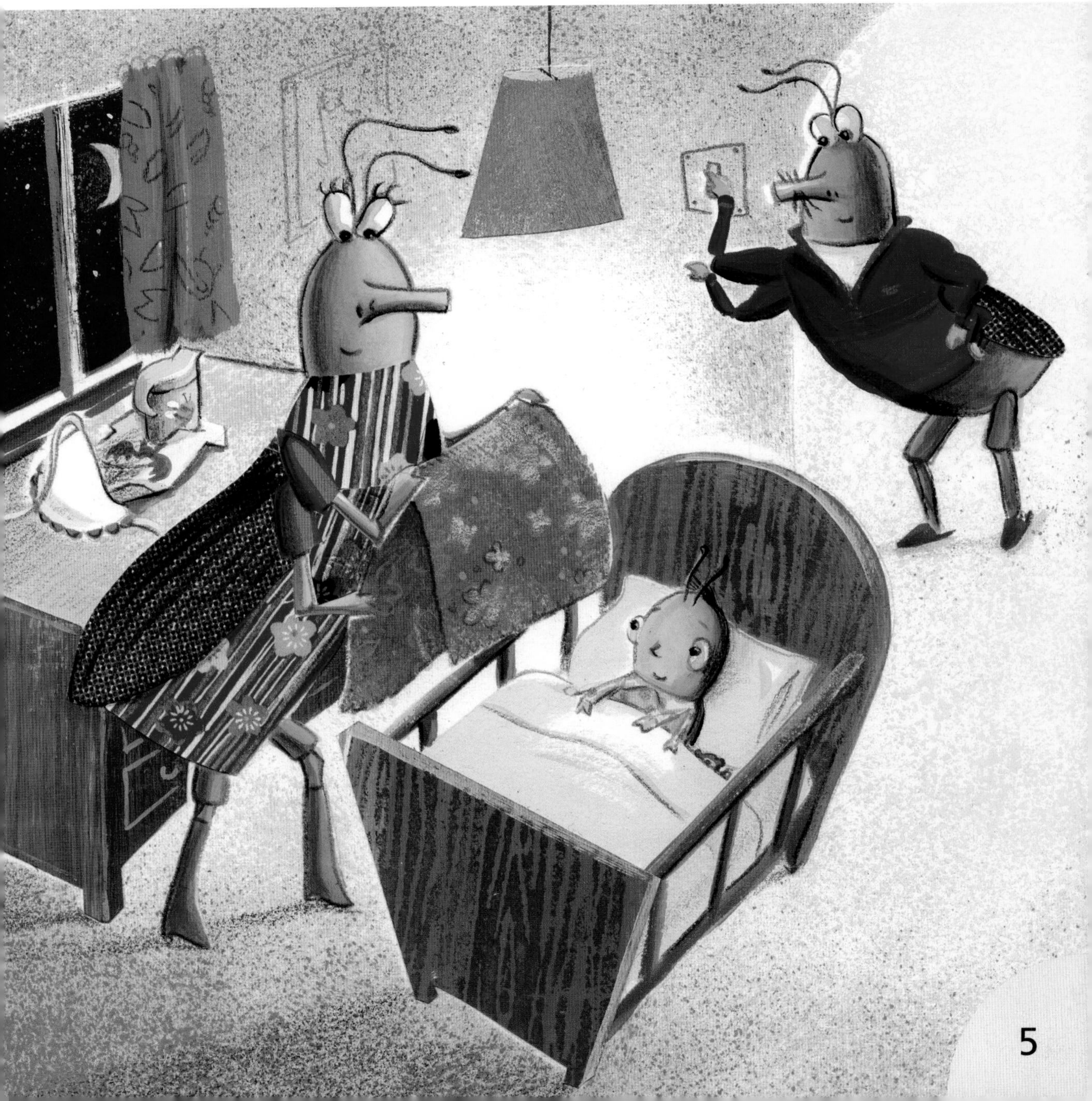

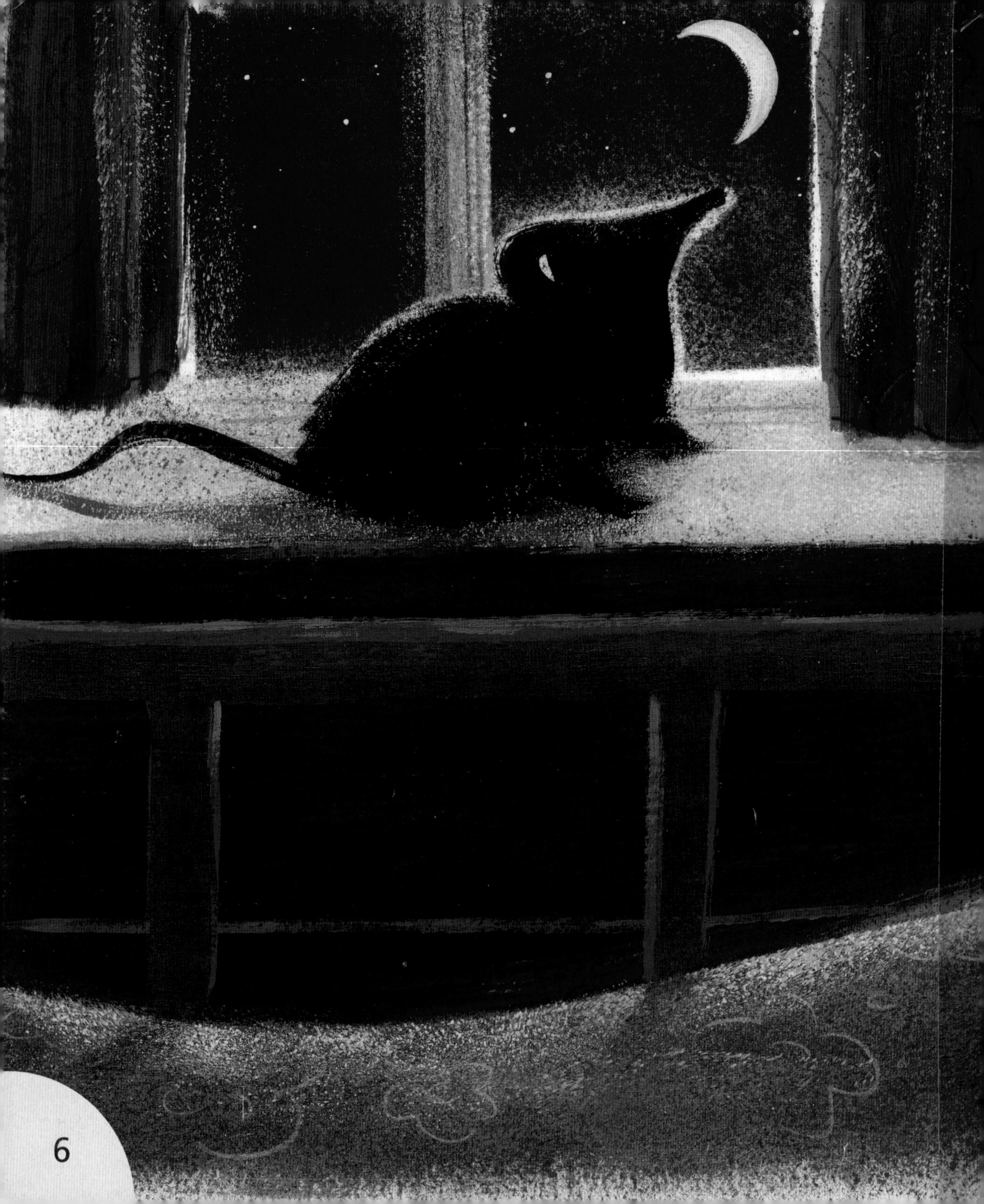

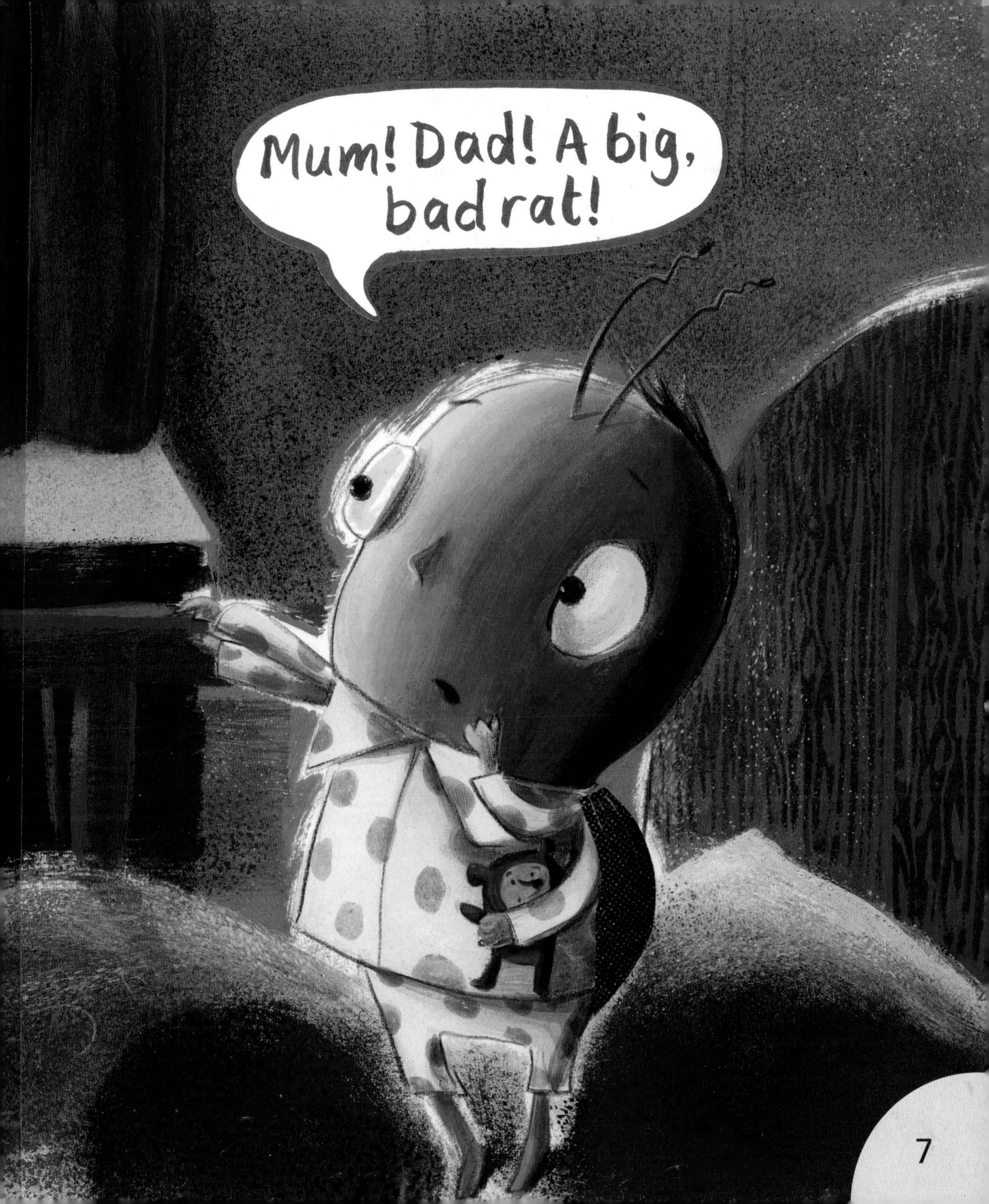
Mum! Dad! A big, bad rat!

Bob Bug has a hug.

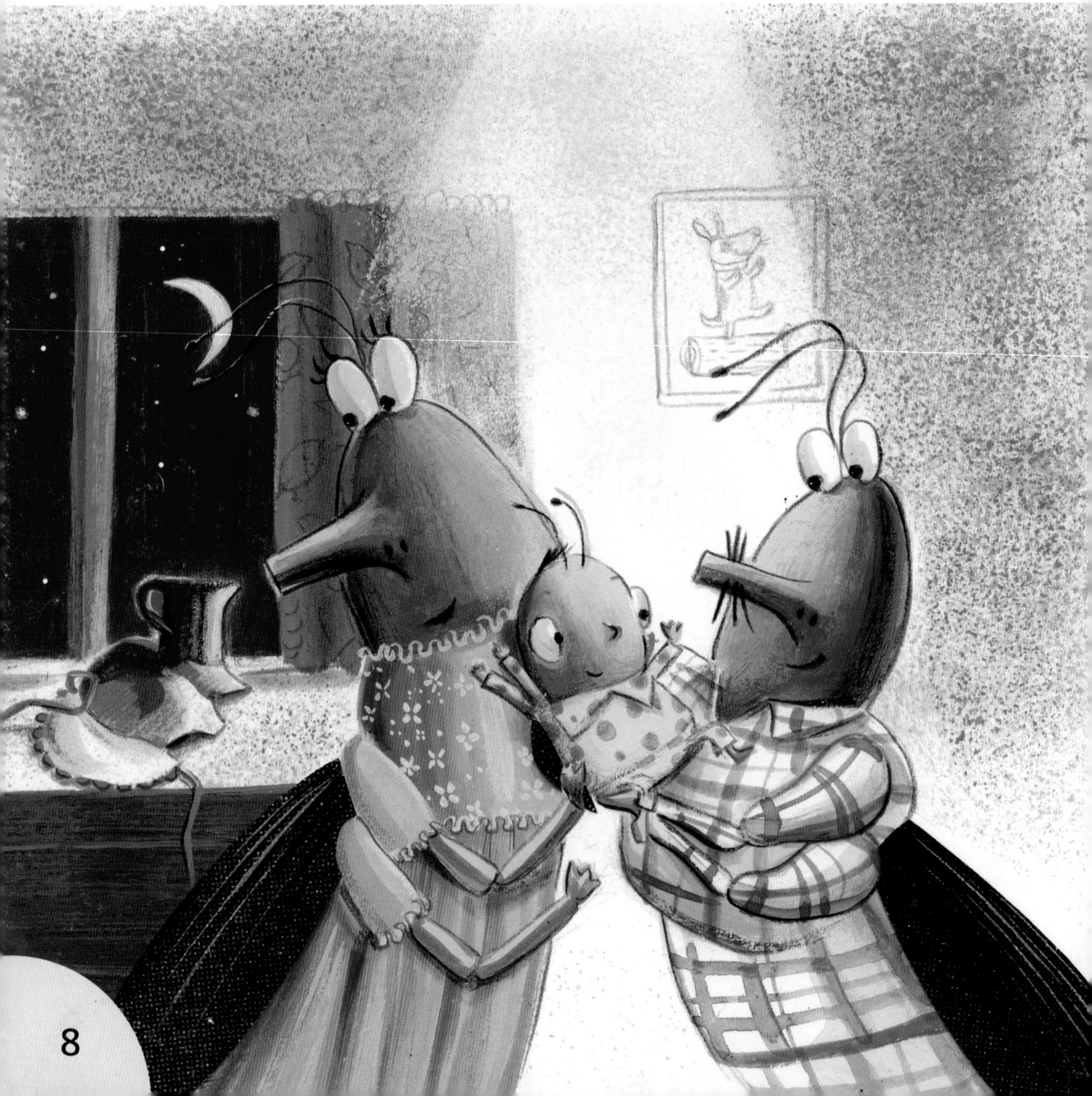